turn the clocks upside down

poetry

aoife mannix

tall-lighthouse

to Sarah

The author wishes to thank the following: Adisa, Janie Armour, Apples & Snakes, Malika Booker, British Council, Central Foundation School for Girls, Creative Partnerships, Geraldine Collinge, Natalie Cook, Simon Cook, Cathy Fitzgerald, Mark Hewitt, Mike Kirchner, Hilary Kneale, HsinYi Ku, Deirdre McCarthy, National Gallery, Joan O'Connell, Sinead Russell, Cathy Ryan, Andy Scorzelli, Shihue Tu, Kerry Bradley, Michale Chang, Sandy Chi, Rosa Conrad, Jeff Ellis, Medway Fuse Festival, Mary Naughton, Nii Parkes, Malika's Poetry Kitchen, Theatre de Complicité, Heather Tyrrell & my family.

Acknowledgements are due to the editors of the following magazines & publications in which some of these poems first appeared: Asian Journal, Citizen 32, Creature Magazine, Ledbury Festival, Manual of Domestic Incidents, Medway Fuse Festival, National Gallery Podcast, Trespass, Nth position.

Cover image by Chloë Barter

Cover photo of Aoife Mannix © Andy Rumball

Cover design from an original concept by Suman

© 2008
Aoife Mannix has asserted her rights under the Copyright, Design & Patents Act 1988 to be identified as the author of this work.

published 2008
ISBN 978 1 904551 55 3
www.tall-lighthouse.co.uk

contents

Late	1
Paddling	2
In the New Forest	3
Wonder Woman	4
Cathedral	5
Tessellating	6
Scare	7
Explanations	8
Costa Rica	9
Active	10
Pura Vida	11
Searching	12
Priceless	13
Street of Tolerance, Berlin	14
Snow in Taiwan	15
A night out in Taipei	16
Paiwan	18
Xue Xue	19
The Notebook	20
Going back to Bangkok	21
Time Lords	22
By the creek	23
The paintings at night	24
Prague	26
Are we nearly there yet?	27
Children of men	28
A disappearing number	30
Burma	31
Bad news	32
St Pancras	33
Spooks	34
Jazz	35
Haunted	36
Soi Cowboy, Bangkok	37
Not just S&M	38
Dream	39
God Bless the Child	40
Gift	42

Wonderful	43
Buried	44
A house for all seasons	46
Demolition	48
Tracks	49
Treasure	50
Daffodils	51
Help	52
Worship	53
Naval Heritage	54
We are here	55
Boats	56
Hospice	57
Journey	58
Why I love train journeys	59
Vienna	60
Miles Davis said to John Coltrane...	61
Birth	62
Mass	63
Fashion statement	64
Conscience	66
Advice	67

*If you can't read these scribblings
I'll print my translation in invisible ink,
make it more than waterproof,
all journeys being lost, all words
open to interpretation,
all history selective.*

Late

There are too many words in my head,
feverish red flowers that bloom through
patches of sunlight. If music is the writing
of tombstones then the songs have too many
memories; layers of paint, flashes of other
dances, lyrics I no longer remember. The air
whistling through my lungs is off tune, iced
with the smoke of all that I have been.
It can't go any slower, I burn
and burn through the ticking of hours,
the star charts of unspoken prophesies
where Venus is always rising.
I want to be able to read your future.
This note I strike in the face of history,
in the face of the loss that is coming,
even though I know not one of these rhymes
can give or take a single second
or be half as beautiful as your father's speech
at your birthday party. He spoke of
waiting for you when we knew he was dying,
how tiny and fragile a baby you were,
late yet premature, such contradictions
are written into our horoscopes.

Paddling

The shock of September sunshine
as Indian skies smile down on us,
years stripped bare, as if those
small town winters never happened,
as if I'd never thought of walking
into the waves on Christmas Eve
with my pockets full of sleeping pills,
no taxi fare, or even the name
of a destination to keep me afloat.

It's funny the things I have forgotten;
glass bottles with small bones inside,
that time I broke my toe and limped
through the halls of the dying
in my father's oversized shoes,
wincing at my own stupidity,
thinking isn't it hilarious
how nothing is ever so bad,
that it can't get worse.

I'd no idea then how water heals,
how to breathe the air of your ocean
could clean salt from my blood
and put laughter back into my veins.
If I tell you I've been broken,
will you believe in my walking
and let me bathe in the beauty
I see reflected in the blue of your past?

The water is cold but clear,
my feet no longer afraid
to leave their prints
on the clean slate of our future,
this love I could swim for,
never mind autumn's warning
or the shortness of the light.

In the New Forest

Light pours late summer between the trees,
pools of warmth splash amongst the hush of green
as I watch you scaling the branches,
an echo of laughter clicking in camera poses,
instant kisses exposed as the absence of raindrops.
I struggle to absorb the quality of oxygen,
not sure I've the strength for this happiness.

In the distance, I catch a glimpse of a Shetland pony
stepping through a spot of sunlight, his legs
impossibly short. My kind of unicorn.
I want to take him home and keep him
in the garden shed. I know it's not possible
but at least I'm breathing again.

As if some of the lightness of your smile
has reached the darker corners of my lungs,
my throat no longer filled with wood,
my skin less likely to catch fire,
my footsteps dappled and shining,
dancing along a stream of golden afternoon
as you take my hand, soft as August.

Wonder Woman

If you see me in my vast array of suitcases,
tattered excuses, wrapped in tomorrow's
newspaper headlines, dreaming in a doorway,
my mouth full of spare change and my pockets
on fire, a chameleon that's forgotten how
to change colour, the rain nibbling at my bones,
it's only my own fur I'm wearing, this hedgehog
tuxedo, my faith in fool's gold, my unfathomable
belief in mirages in the desert, Father Christmas
and the tooth fairy.

Please don't judge me too harshly, I'm just
trying to practice my super powers,
it takes concentration to be invisible,
to be so small I'm untouchable,
to shoot spiders webs from my hands.
I never did learn to lie with any style
and why can't I find a phone box when I need one?

Maybe you could help me to stop dialling
the wrong number, to figure out my left from my right,
to avoid falling down rabbit holes, to quit all those
eat-me-drink-me compulsive hallucinations,
to find a skin that fits me. I'm so weary of
costume changes, early morning flights,
missing sequins, my panda eyes,
these brittle vodka nights, the truth reflected
in a bottle. Never mind about terms
and conditions, I'm through with skipping ropes.
I'm not looking for a hero, I just wondered
if there's any chance you'd let me follow you home?

Cathedral

I step out of the prism of platinum lies
to find myself no longer reflected
through the glass shards of your lack of faith
whispered through blues and reds and greens
as death is protested in the street.

I sit looking out at the lighthouse
with my lungs chipped and polished.
In the shipwreck of this loss
I feel the wind of healing ghosts
in the memory of her hands.

Even if it has taken all this time,
there is a chance that, in spite of myself,
I might yet taste the colour
of something close to grace.

Tessellating

You send me that picture
I managed to take
on your mobile phone.
Even though I'm no photographer,
by some magic of the morning light
I've caught you golden
as I see you when you're sleeping.

If you look close enough
you can make out
the shadow of my smile
curled between your breasts
as you dare me to click
the phrase multiple orgasm,
or that other expression
I can never remember
for how my hip fits into yours,
jigsaw puzzles in my own private gallery.

I'm developing kisses
in a sealed darkroom,
watching them emerge
in black and white.
As I hang them up to dry
I focus whole new colours
in this kaleidoscope
as the pieces tumble and fall
in their secret significance.

Scare

We are all afraid here.
It's the waiting that grinds the teeth.
Just the phrase *test results*
holds so many dreaded pauses;
an exam we've long ago failed,
DNA decoded, how cells erode,
capsize and flower in ways
that were never intended.
Her heart no longer in the right place,
the macabre humour of surgical knives,
what they cut out, what they left in,
growth can be such a deadly word.

The slight echo on the phone line,
the gaps of long distance silence,
my father's voice repeating
what he couldn't say;
that I am his messenger.
We've been to this place before,
know we will go there again,
but for now the sirens sound the all clear
and I breathe deep this momentary closeness,
how we are oddly united in the face of fear.

Explanations

If I could define this moment
in my own language
you'd be able to taste
the fifteen different words for snow
because my fear of dictionaries
is not the same as my fear of history;
the weight of those other afternoons
crammed with the junk
of what I thought I needed.

Sometimes to escape is a kind of cleansing,
what gets washed away is more than words,
the grime of too many compromises,
how dust is ninety-eight percent psychotic.

I'm terrified of being lost again
or following a map I don't believe in,
searching for my own invisible city,
a space time warp of lucidity
when the whole grid lights up
and the connections are not at all
what anybody said they would be.

Instead of grand philosophies
there's the silence of snow crystals on your skin,
their patterns etched in an eternal instant.
Maybe I've always been in two places at once,
maybe you are moving near the speed of light.
I trace angels across your body,
the rhythm underneath the signposts,
listening for your sense of direction
as simple as singing your heartbeat.

Costa Rica

We arrive where jade gods
are carved as roaring jaguars
that spring from clay jungles
as snakes hiss a purity of the soul.
The tombs of civilisations interrupted,
their stories glistening in gold blood
where the Spanish found their way out of San Jose,
the greed of gringos tastes bitter in the bananas,
the CIA pulls its puppet strings, the signs
point out child prostitution is illegal.

But this piece of fierce green
has escaped military heritage,
the coffee tastes of peace
and dazzling waterfalls,
the rain sweeps rivers before us,
a fragile arc of colour stretching
glimpses through the clouds
as we stand before the mist of the mountains.

Active

The man in the bright orange shirt
selling razor blades and hand guns
as the bus belches onto a Swiss cheese
road. There is the promise of lava,
hot liquid cocktails in steaming spas
as we float off our bar stools.

The volcano is wrapped in the knowledge
that one day its breath will sweep away
all these paper umbrellas,
it rumbles how we are nothing
but fragile kisses lost in the mist
as night cracks open the world,
at the centre of it all there is only fire,
broken, angry, biding its time.

Yet now in this whirlpool,
your skin soft as the rainforest
retreating into its own strange
spark of fireflies, a flint struck
in the face of the dark,
the gentle hush of you
sleeping beside me,
the greenness of this adventure,
the earth holding still.

Pura Vida

Here where the waves crash white as snow
the blue heron spikes his punk hairdo,
the iguana sports an orange Mohawk,
the water turns mercury jade
as the boat inches closer
to crocodile eyes, watching, always watching
as we slide through this jungle circus.

The vividness of feather trapeze artists
tumbling across the sky,
echoing whoops of fire cries
from some surreal orchestra
as the forest tunes up for breakfast.

We are the freaks in our own freak show
sharing beer with a leaf disguised as a cricket,
there are no words in the dictionary
for the sheer green of our applause.

I spell your tiger wings with the missing letters
of what I wanted to tell you
about the wonder of turtles,
reflected happiness, the sky inverted,
all worries the foolishness of clowns,
the cities of painted faces further away
than we ever believed possible.

Your footprints are carved
on the flip side of my ocean
along a beach created for nesting,
this long rush to reach the sea,
we have made it at last,
eggs cracked, a shell for a home.

Searching

The gigantic ceiling fan spins the shadow
of our last hours in the sun, golden and mellow
on the broken streets as we wander through
the earthquake damaged cathedral
and the old woman asks what we're looking for?

I could not begin to answer, but as the hills
fall over each other into the sea
it occurs to me that I've never been able
to see so far into the future, to feel
the earth solid beneath my feet, to know
the corners will not be snatched from me.

The startling purple of flowers draped across a wall
is no more shocking than the blue of your eyes
reflecting my glimpse of the ocean
from the tightest curl of the highest mountain road
sliced through a rainforest on the edge of love.

Priceless

The heat eases from the day.
As the sun slides down the sky
the hypnotic rhythm of waves
lulls us into another space,
free of dictionary anxiety where the words
build mountains between us.

I collect your memories as broken seashells
because you do not like to speak of sickness
or the guilt of snow when you stood accused
of a crime that has no spelling.

Love seeks its own asylum.

If we do not attempt to ride the waves
how can we know the taste of salt?
The elegance of perfect pitch,
the sand worn fine with question marks,
the freedom to be who we really are,
birthdays in the jungle.

A return to the wilderness of ourselves
before we were trimmed
and hedged in by petty expectations,
the need to force all kisses into currency
as if the oceans did not count for wonder.

Street of Tolerance, Berlin

It's the surprise of quiet Saturday streets,
even though the sky is heavy with history
as we wind through the silent faces of stone.
The thinness of sculptured shadows
who made journeys no one should have to take,
a brutal transformation from old age to cattle trucks,
arbitrary barbed wire, a wall of graffiti pebbles,
streets broken in two as the floodgates opened up
the television and the jigsaw pieces bruised flesh.

Now we wait for the rain to pass,
sip coffee dreams and talk about lost babies,
the price of knowing who you are.
Do orphans ever learn their own name?
After the war the priests refused
to give the baptised children back,
as if Jesus had never walked on water
and all we'd learned is to put bricks between us.

Shoot on sight no man's land,
a wounded boy unclaimed,
the crumbled stars of smashed failure,
the taste of earth in our mouths.

The mountains of hate whipped away,
the crane swinging dangerously near,
the transparency of a perfect cloud.
Is it possible to ever remember
what a buried stone means?

If I was a building, I'd be the shaded absence
of trees hidden away inside an invisible city,
the streaming of birds across a metallic sky,
eagle statues free of their violent grandeur.

Snow in Taiwan

There are snowflakes tied to the window
but it's not as warm as you'd expect
as I flash past screaming neon
and try to imagine myself translated into Chinese;
how the symbols make building blocks of the rain
and there is no alphabetical order,
the sounds themselves are pictures
as I discover I am the year of the mouse
but have no idea what that means.

In the swirling red yellow cut out prints
of a new year sculpted in stone,
pigs smile and wink their golden fortune,
the rice itself has a spirit of wildness
splashed black and white across
the whole length of the café.
I look out on the tallest building on earth
trying to read the minimalism of time,
discover how surprisingly easy it is
to turn the clocks upside down,
rearrange the passage of years,
find new calendars.

A night out in Taipei

What I taste most is the kindness
as I squeeze ancient Chinese wisdom
into a cup of hot water
and swirl my oxygen dreams
against cubic squares of light.

You can buy bottles of unconditional love
from a twenty-four hour supermarket here.
A young man gives me a gift of his words
even though he knows I cannot read them.
By this time even I've started to forget
I don't speak Mandarin
as smiles are seamlessly translated
and names tell their own story.

They don't think about the missiles
pointed at them, at least not much,
even though there is no direct connection
and to get a visa she would have to say
she is someone she is not,
so she avoids the mainland.

Our island tragedies share unlikely echoes,
how much are we prepared to lay claim to ourselves
and whether it's really worth dying over?
These choices have eaten up my country too.

We swap tales of other cities,
Paris, Berlin, New York,
being shouted at in the street,
how Europeans hate each other,
how Americans are too arrogant for that.

How mothers always think the world
so much smaller and more dangerous than it is,
the glass violence of the television,
something universal about fear
and as I slide into the yellow taxi
thinking of you, perhaps love too,
perhaps love too.

Paiwan

She asks me why I don't write in my own language,
a question that would take centuries to answer
but one that still wakes me in the night
as I feel my tongue alien in my mouth
and wonder what else besides the words got lost.

When history has you born speaking like a foreigner
you cling to the magic of mispronunciations,
the awkwardness of vowel sounds,
it's not just tonal, it's angry, how a part of me
wants my name to stick in their throat,
needs to believe that the music is still there
underneath the translation.

It's the sound of resistance,
the beating of feet on a wooden floor,
the spell of story telling, the echo
of older voices flowing through the chanting,
those special silent spaces beyond mere words.

Xue Xue

I choose the tiniest teapot on earth for you.

She claims this can serve ten people
in miniature china cups.

Everything here is so elegant
that the doors disappear into the walls.

She spreads her vagrant love letters on the table,
carefully painted heartbreak in beautiful characters

as the boy in the kimono sings classical Taiwanese
and I imagine his Marilyn Monroe wig.

She helps him tie a pink bow and hide behind
the foliage. There is a ladder stretching up beyond

the organic menus to symbolise MSN messenger clichés
and she sings in translation of missing the future

as everyone dances to aboriginal drum beats.

The Notebook

We get the train into Manhattan.
The skyscrapers scratch my breath away
but my mother thinks the taxi drivers
unforgivably rude. We go to
Barnes & Noble bookstore,
the biggest bookshop I have ever seen.

She says I can pick any notebook I want,
beginning a life long obsession with stationery.
I stroke the clean silk of white pages,
smell the stitching of words unwritten
as if they were already there in invisible ink.

I settle on a deep reddish purple,
hard backed but soft to the touch,
my mother doesn't even look at the price
which is something of a first as she tells
the startled man behind the counter
It's for my daughter, for her writing.

Going back to Bangkok

It's the feeling of vertigo I remember most
as I stare out at lights floating into the distance,
the skytrain snaking through the night.
The menu at my favourite noodle bar
is exactly the same, it's me
that's no longer in disguise
as I pick my way through street sellers
and students in crisp white shirts,
the inversion of amnesia,
like the memories I have are not my own.

A building site transformed
into a hotel with nineteen floors
even though I've seen
how they undertake construction
with bamboo poles, no safety hats
and there are cracks in the airport runways.

I think of knocking on a door at six in the morning
to complain about the constant hammering,
only to have my anger collapse
at the sight of twelve year old boys drilling holes
in the walls for twelve hours a day, and it's clear
from the unmade sofa that they sleep here too.

I wonder if the miniature shanty town
in the shadow of the magnificent department store
is still spreading despite the lack of running water
and the kids playing football in a rubbish dump.

Time Lords

I come from a broken place;
my father in his dressing gown
leaning against the radiator for warmth,
a half drunk glass of red wine on the table,
my brother with his shirt open to exhaustion.

For half an hour or more we discuss the wonders
of Dr Who, the TARDIS and the creepy music at the end.
My father tells me he never knew I found it terrifying
as a child, had to retreat to the kitchen to drink cups
of tea with my Nana with the spectre of Daleks
threatening to exterminate us in the background.
Who would believe now that a sink plunger
could hold such terror?

My father believes in technology,
I believe in imagination, though special effects
like chemotherapy have leeched our fragile faith.
My brother finds the new series with the gas masks
and the zombies pleading for their mothers
a feat of psychological genius.

For half an hour or more we agree with each other,
the kitchen lamp bathes our enthusiasm, the clock
has lost its lethal ticking, we are in a space far bigger
than it seems on the outside.

By the creek

The kingfisher flashes startling blue
over lagoon green water,
skimming the breeze
as a single leaf falls
in a slow waltz,
a ship sailing across
an ocean of jade tranquillity.

Butterflies herald
this orange-black
dancing procession.

Small fish skate near the surface
as I sit on the end of the jetty
in my own secret world
dreaming under the richness
of a turquoise sky.

The peace dappled through the branches
is warm with the promise of morning,
as if time itself were just a hawk circling,
such grace, such silence.

The paintings at night

The sense of relief when the last of the squalling groups
troop out with their gum cracking teenage laughter.
Little old ladies who linger, as if being closer
to the other side they suspect that once the doors close
the eyes that seem to be watching are more than
tricks of shadow and light, the imprisonment
of lost souls painted into corners.

Their expressions no longer frozen, but flowing
along the walls in whispered rushes of gold and white,
a riot of colours racing through light sensitive halls,
the air brushed with centuries of stories. The dust
of all portraits is ninety-nine percent human skin.

We slip in and out of the landscapes,
their swirling impressions of pathways
leading deep into other worlds
as we breathe our mythic conversations,
a language of starry nights and crucifixions.

Doorways within doorways,
the magic of time travel after midnight
when the gardens breathe shifting skies,
the horse gallops free from the frame
and we are no longer a single expression,
a moment frozen, but all the hundreds of years
that have danced in the moonlight.

We echo to each other; who suffered most,
who sat for longest, who's been restored,
who got hidden during the war,
who's been painting of the month,
turned into a postcard, reprinted
and sold a million times, catalogued,
downloaded, our faces pressed and contorted.

It seemed like flattery once, but in the hushed
quiet of our own eternal night, we can't help
resent all this endless watching.
We never realised life is just a rough sketching
but now find we are layers and layers
of everyone who ever looked at us,
paused and stopped and saw something fragile
in the blue of a dress, the playfulness of a smile,
who saw us naked for who we are, ghosts
in the woodwork, trapped love stories, pearl
oceans, moments of reflection, haunting
the lives of those we seek to portray.

Prague

Strolling by the river with the water cascading
and the giant chair on the edge of tipping over,
the bridges curve through each other
as the tiny bird hides in the hedge,
skeleton puppets locked into stone,
wooden sculptures knarled with question marks,
a jazz metamorphosis, the dark cigar cellars
of golden beer and classical paranoia.

The boats churning ducks
as I remember the taste of *zmrzlina,*
flickers of happiness, melting borders,
the American asking for grass
and prophesizing a city sold for a song,
he strummed his guitar, organised spy tours,
said the Czechs would come to regret capitalism.

Now the Persil automatic mural is gone,
the tanks no longer pink,
the revolution no longer velvet
but rough under the tongue,
the cost of art, faces printed on a short skirt.

Jokes that carried prison sentences,
not knowing what your crime was,
the aftertaste of betrayal
as the colour seeps back in,
history in the reflection of sunshine on water.

Walking back over the bridge,
the puppets nudge each other,
corruption mutates,
bureaucracy loves bullet holes.

Are we nearly there yet?

On the train the man across from me
is talking to his two little girls,
the smallest, so small she fits
snugly against the window frame,
counts how many stops there are to go.
Her older sister corrects her with the superiority
of those for whom counting is no longer a wonder.
They are about to argue when their father says
don't worry about it; the stops are always changing,
it's not so far now, I'll tell you when we get there.

And I think of my father, on long summer drives
across the west of Ireland, with the light fading
and the green brokenness of the land,
that time we saw the truck overturn
in a huge orange ball
and though we begged him to pull over
so we could gasp at the flames,
he refused, saying it's not our destination,
some things you don't yet need to see,
and he kept on driving us all the way home.

Children of men

The last of the light plays on the wall
to the rhythm of summer evenings,
your face so still and far from me
as I ask what's wrong, and you say
nothing, nothing at all.

Just that in waiting for the ship to come in,
the gentle lapping of the waves,
those final moments before the credits roll
and the last baby on earth is saved,
you suddenly saw your own death
clear as steam wiped from a mirror.

A small hole in the fabric of time,
unstitched, fallen, the ruins of an earthquake
or the black and white flickering of soldiers
running over the lip of history.

Did they know they'd always be a silent newsreel?
Swallowed up, washed out by exposure,
their features seeped away, till they are mainly smoke
curling from a cigarette or a blur of mud,
the occasional red poppy worn for decoration.

If in Japan they build their foundations on fault lines,
do they smudge lipstick backwards in the mirror,
feel the terror of their skulls under the thinnest of skin
or is it simply more honest to know that earth buckles,
that clocks are not solid, that the seconds tumble
from our lips raw as star ulcers, and not one
single kiss can be added or subtracted
from the sum of our stone total.

Though I make you promise not to die,
for this time you might not come back,
I know it is a lie sure as nightfall,
sure as the street lamps switching on
to mark the end of day,
their orange glow a mechanical ritual
that says the light is gone and we are shadows,
nothing at all, just shadows.

A disappearing number

Sometimes in the closing of a door,
in the power of dividing by zero,
in the silences of there being no answer,
I think of your ashes,
bone turned to snowflakes.
You said remember we're just chalk
and into chalk we must return.

There is no theorem for love,
though some eternities
are bigger than others,
the stars play their own music
tied to parallel strings,
the counting of a heart beat,
contradictory rhythms
as simple as a nursery rhyme,
what will remain of us
is the beauty of nothing.

A man surviving on apples,
absence becoming presence,
the distance light travels.
We can never touch the dead
no matter how close the fractions get,
that is the cruelty of mathematics,
the loneliness of gravitational pull.

But if time is a cheap card trick,
if there are other universes
where we've never met,
I still say one plus one equals three.
A child is not a square root, an easy equation,
it's about the patterns a day makes,
what the eye creates, a match struck in the dark.

Burma

A body tied to a tree. The constant drip of water.
The monks erased in their orange robes.
Helicopter arms hung from a ceiling fan.
The motorcycle position.
A torturer's sense of humour.
Human mine clearance;
what it means to walk across borders,
to take to the streets when the lady's name
never rises above a whisper.
The man with the newspaper is listening,
its pages only camouflage,
headlines crushed
while oil flows slick with hypocrisy.
A country buried alive.
Buddha shot taking a photograph.
A conscience riddled with the missing.
The blood of unknown statistics.
Chinese dollars.
The passing of the buck.
Apologies for sanctifying murder.
We turn away into silence
betraying the reincarnation of hope.

Bad news

Today I heard a boy I kissed
twenty years ago committed suicide.
I don't remember much about him
apart from the fact he was always laughing.

All these years I haven't thought of him
and even his own brother had no idea why he did it
but the shadow of sad, angry young men
fills me with unease; heroin addiction,
punches thrown in the dark, the look
on your face in that last photograph.

That scar on your forehead,
the mark of where I dropped you.
I stand accused of knowing too little and too much.
You said you hoped one day to meet her again.
Do the dead remember us?

I haven't got an answer to these questions.
You claimed I was the one that got away
but sometimes I slip through a chink in time,
back to a classroom with a boy
winking at me, cheeky and confident,
a joker, a suicidal clown.

St Pancras

The train journey has been cut short,
something to do with wheels turning,
the width of the tracks,
as the girl in emerald shoes
knocks back her tequila,
thinking of tornadoes
and marrying in a hurry,
how much sea we can go under.

A question of passion and visas,
another way to travel
as the ukulele orchestra tunes up,
the chords scrawled across the map of the world,
you are my sunshine, my only sunshine.
I sit suspended on a bar stool
noticing how the lighting has changed
but all the old heartbreak is still here.

Outside the rain relentlessly wipes
the smiles off tired faces,
the hoardings shiver closer.
They've rearranged the roads,
but I wander through pink tinted puddles,
surprisingly sober making excellent time,
yet you're not pleased to see me,
the connection has been missed.

Spooks

For a second your eyes are stripped
of all secret identities, you are a small child
playing spies, the excitement of mysterious
codes, undercover missions.

If we could go deep into the heart of the Kremlin,
share our nuclear technology, listening devices,
I'd give you my licence to kill, pour endless
martinis as we discuss arms deals,
how to smuggle heroin, save the world.

I'd be your translator, bodyguard,
the one that never betrays you,
I'd wait for you in public places
pretending to be strangers
as we swapped briefcases,
I'd issue you with a new passport,
invent you a secret weapon.

We'd go to all the casinos, crack dens,
whore houses, we'd be shot at, stabbed,
poisoned, kidnapped and tortured,
but we'd know we were destined to survive
because we're the heroes of this thriller.

Jazz

The glass elevator saxophone shatters,
the earthquake in the bar rocks crimson lust,
drums ripple into crumpled silk
as you and I catch the Metro
all the way into the kiss of Paris.

Bottles roll to the floor,
there are broken notes
crunching under our dancing feet,
the ground swallows us whole,
we are the music, the music
is the end of the world,
rich deep red, longing for more.

Haunted

You dream with open eyes.
It frightens me in the night
when you see strangers
crawling from the ceiling.
I think of rowing across the stars,
those who come back from the other side
as if the walls of consciousness
were not solid, only doors
opening and closing with the ghosts
of those who never really left,
still out there on the edge of memory,
a face at the window,
a tree tapping,
the light switched on.

Soi Cowboy, Bangkok

You'll know it by the gigantic neon boot
hanging over the mouth of the street,
the flashing stripes of good times guaranteed
and of course the girls in their thigh-high cowboy boots,
black hair tied tight in pigtails,
hats silver and red with buckaroo stars,
ropes that have never caught cattle,
only sweaty Western men in their obscene t-shirts,
salivating and jet lagged with their flies undone
and their eyes full of rodeo rides.

It's always the same, except at Christmas
when the girls sport Santa Claus caps instead,
and if you look closer you can see that John Wayne
is not a man she'd ever care to meet given the choice,
unless he plans to come by on his white horse
and *yee hah* her out of this world of mirror balls,
greasy poles, amphetamines, cheap whisky
and cheaper sex.

You can tell by the ancient look in her under age eyes
that Cowboys and Indians is not a game she wants
to be playing, but it's not her frontier and it's always
the natives that get scalped.

Not just S&M

If I could tie
you up with vowels,
pin you to the bed
with the force of my metaphor,
strip away your similes,
get down on my hands and knees
and crawl across your consonants,
whip you with verbs,
cover you with adjectives,
lick the poetry from your skin,
pierce your secrets,
tattoo love letters between your legs,
graffiti your breasts,
sign my name along your tongue,
if I could make love to you
using every single letter
of the alphabet, I would.

Dream

I'm remembering being in America
when I was fifteen years old
and Andy and Lance and all their talk
of taking a motorbike and driving right across
all the way to California,
and the jackets they'd wear,
and the way the road would smell,
and the grease and the sweat and the mountains,
and how they'd drink beer
and maybe even go down to Mexico,
and it'd be cool and free.

I'm wondering if they ever made that trip
so I put their names into Google twenty years later,
what comes up is pictures of boats,
Andy is standing on one called *Nightingale*.
I can't be sure it's him, but I like to think it is,
and now he's a salmon fisherman in Alaska
with photos of rainbows and ice,
and Lance is also a sea captain,
gone organic and feeding polar bears.
Maybe it's two other boys altogether,
but logging off, I feel strangely reassured,
as if something stayed true in spite of it all.

God Bless the Child

The last time I saw you, you were singing
your bones out in some seedy Las Vegas club,
gold peeling off the walls and the sound turned
down so as not to disturb the clink of slot machines.
You threw your arms around me saying
I was the first real human being you'd seen since
you got there. I wanted to grab you and put you
in my suitcase, I wanted to tell you there's
more than one way to hang a woman,
but then again who knew that better than you
as you shot the blues straight into your veins,
knocked back a bottle of pure truth every day,
even when they wouldn't let you sit at the bar.

They swung your lyrics from the trees
but they were afraid of the storms in your eyes,
and even when you lay dying, they kept watch
in case you might rise phoenix like from the bed,
the most powerful of jailbirds set free,
and the roar of your voice would burn them
with the crying shame of their lynch mob mentality.
They took away your flowers, your radio,
trying to kill you with the pettiness of their hatred.

They found a few hundred dollars taped to your body
and seventy five cents in your bank account, you had
spent your last dime feeding the starving ghost of jazz,
smoky saxophone nights that cracked hearts into pieces
all so that we could escape the dawn. Lady Day
who only lived the nights packed with notes rougher
than diamonds cut from the rock of American apartheid.
You can't segregate music, all of us have ears,
but not all of us are listening. The cries of an eleven
year old child being raped, a fourteen year old
prostitute. It pays to know the price of things.

They banned you from every club in New York,
refused to record your song about the bitterness
of a Southern breeze, locked you up for over a year,
but who's the criminal here? You whisper to me,
*the thing is, they can't put policemen inside a record
groove.* The crackle of your voice still mocking
them with its priceless dignity. '*Papa may have,
mama may have, but God bless the child that's got his own.*'

Gift

When I was a child
looking through the picture book
my mother said to me
pick any word you want
and it's yours for eternity,
I will give it to you in all its translation.
I chose the word strawberry,
fresh and softly melting in my mouth.
She said if you take this world
one mouthful at a time,
you'll find it's far sweeter,
the sugar mixed with cream,
the pink swirling in the white.

Years later we sat in the sun
eating strawberries,
my mother said this is the life.

The doctors spoke their own language
but we never managed to learn it.
She said if she could pick one word
it would be hope, that's not
asking for so much surely.
But we had run out of letters,
and neither of us knew how to spell
the afternoon into forever.

Wonderful

I think that's wonderful,
really I do, just wonderful.
How amazing, I mean just great,
good for you, really good for you.
I mean men are just a waste of space anyway
when you think about it.
I think you're totally right,
really I do…
I kissed a girl once,
yes in college for a dare,
of course our boyfriends were watching,
it was just a silly dare, long time ago…
And I'm sure she must be wonderful too,
your girlfriend, a really fantastic person,
and you must be so happy together,
really it's just fantastic…
I've no problem with it at all,
I mean why would it bother me?
No I think it's great, really great,
really, really great,
just wonderful…

Buried

I have never been to visit her grave,
perhaps there is a part of me
that doesn't want to know,
or see again that narrow strip of green
beside a brutal highway
with the whispering of traffic
and the mountains cut against the sky.

I have enough ghosts already.
They catch their reflections
in the bottom of teacups,
the repetitions of mirrors,
the echoes of songs,
her voice engraved in stone.

Like the time I opened up
that old story book
to find myself a child again
pressed close against her warmth,
the shadow of a lamp across her face,
the picture of a changeling
leaping from roof to roof.

The past is always reaching out to grab me,
greedy and cruel. I slam myself shut to it,
but still she rattles the windows
as I taste the blood of my own fear,
history repeated, a cancerous banshee,
the part of me that is still in that hospital room
with the chemicals dripping
and the walls peeling away
in thin strips of defeat.

I wear these bandages
to keep the insides from falling out.
They made her shroud from a dress
she'd once lent me,
gave me her bracelets to keep,
some strange inheritance.
I have yet to decipher their patterns of gold.

A house for all seasons

In summer I would swing slow arcs
of hammock afternoons,
sipping banana milkshakes
with the soft swoosh of the waves
washing the beach.
Their eternal rhythm
racing a breeze of butterflies
that sing through the long evenings
as the ghosts of paper
burn across a sky full of wishes.
I would stretch myself across this canvas,
cutting a thousand sunsets
into the wooden beams
as they turn from the innocence
of endless August
to the whispered gold
of September's softness.

The birds dream of going home.
I watch them from my window
writing my name in the steam of Sundays
with the table set only for us
and the wine tasting of summer's end,
the bittersweet nostalgia of a tablecloth
sewn with daisy chain necklaces,
the kind children break easily.

The long white candles are lit
for the sacrifice of snow
falling silently over distant fields.
I stand framed in the doorway of winter,
breathing the crystal cold
clarity of frozen earth,
behind me, the fire
crackles a promise of warmth

and the flames dance their shadows of laughter
across bookshelves filled with
the dreams we have yet to have.

Stretched over the ceiling
there is a map of the world
with hundreds of pins in it
marking our voyage to this safe place,
where the daffodils will soon explode their secrets,
there are strawberries to eat in the garden,
bees humming the beginning of adventures
we have yet to learn the words to.

Demolition

If you chip away my skin
you'll discover a remnant
of Victorian nursery rhymes,
heavy floral roses of embossed love affairs,
cracks of jungle animals stalking the ghosts of walls.

You'll get beneath the creamy white
neutrality of spaces easy to rent,
the blood red stripes of roads dug through memory,
lost fragments of teacups smashed in helpless fury,
stains of sugar thrown in a storm of regret,
their sticky shadow still just barely visible
as fingerprints on a light switch.

The place where my fist went through plaster,
dust heavy on my tongue,
words stripped of their windows,
broken glass embedded in my bones,
toothpaste graffiti, the dental records
of a home unidentifiable,
decapitated staircases,
a thousand places where the rain gets in.

Tracks

Pulling into Grand Central Station,
my face pressed against
the ghost of my own reflection,
I stare out into the dragon smoke magic
of train tracks branching into darkness,
the shadow lives of underground people.

Whole villages that never see the light of day
count time to the rhythm of small wheels turning.

Having long since lost interest in destinations,
their inhabitants speak only
the alphabet of coloured lines,
they ride with the secret knowledge
of tunnels etched onto their eyes
reflecting other worlds beneath
the commuter façade,
the pretence of going places.

Treasure

I can see my father
winding up the garden path
pushing his old bike
with the cats basking on the wall
and my mother framed
in the kitchen window
doing the dishes.

Her smile, the definition
of soda pops in the summer,
all that fizz in glass bottles
of reds and oranges
as we jumped from the swings,
marking how high we could fly
and digging for buried treasure
by the old carriage house.

Smashed chips of emerald ghosts,
myths of crockery,
I polished them carefully
searching for dates,
the magic of faded kings on old coins,
kept them in a wooden box
my mother gave me.

How precious they seemed,
fragments of past lives,
strangers that we ourselves
would one day become.

Daffodils

My father explained how that summer
they bought their dream cottage,
he promised my mother
a riot of colours come spring,
but she just smiled at him,
always more of a realist.

He wanted to prove his faith;
planted them in exact rows
carefully measuring the space
to allow the roots to sink deep,
turning over the soil slowly
so that each one
had its own special bed,
the earth was hard
and cold to his touch,
but he cut at it with a small trowel
till it crumbled and breathed.

My mother watched him working
on his knees the whole afternoon,
he planted them for her, he said,
even though they both knew
there was only the tiniest chance
she'd ever see them.

When he'd finished,
they sat in deckchairs
sipping beer
and eating strawberries.
She held his hand and told him,
let's not worry about the spring,
here now, in this moment,
I can see yellow
everywhere.

Help

We are woken
by a woman screaming.
Three a.m. Her screams
tear through the curtains.
I dial emergency,
try to explain
the quality of fear,
not a drunken brawl
or jealous outrage
but an animal sound
piercing the night.

Ours is the only light
turned on in the street.
As the police car prowls past
to excavate the stuff of nightmares
I imagine all those other sleepers,
the ones whose dreams
carry on regardless,
the ones who are lying there
shrivelling under the covers,
listening to the echo
of their own death
and doing nothing.

Worship

Elephants bearing golden headdresses
weave through the festival of wisdom
as the drums beat tighter
and fireworks explode the night.

More smoke than fire,
but loud enough to stir the spirits
as whole families race past on tiny mopeds
and the horns insist on diving through traffic jams.

Not for the faint hearted
as we speed over the bridge,
worlds connected across time,
how, round the corner,
neon has yet to be invented.

The trees whisper their own ancient languages,
the music of birds flying home into the evening,
their ghost cries lonely splinters
as the breeze kisses our faces
and the hush of a different rhythm
settles into our sighs.

Naval Heritage

The whispered murmur of your breathing,
waves washing against a distant shore.
He picked you up by your ankles,
shocking you back to life, a mermaid creature
come too soon into a world not ready.
Toy penguins kidnapped during the war,
a gift unappreciated, a roll call of ships sunk,
having missed so much land,
how can the years be redrawn?

To navigate love
you need the same compass,
the edges of what can't be said,
more than redecoration, moving on,
St Christopher's medal
to always protect you,
a sailor searching
for some kind of peace.

Home is a relative concept,
dreams passing in the night,
listening for the shipping news,
how to weather these storms in the blood.
You with your smile of adventure,
military precision.
What gets passed on,
defending a nation,
a small child,
fear and courage
in mutual incomprehension.

We are here

This moment of standing on a bridge
staring out at a city bathed in blue
holds us gentle as a wish for happiness.
Even the stones are instruments
as we run to play musical chairs.

There are five pianos
floating at the same time,
the walls of water fall between us.
I tell you how the doctor's voice
took away any hope of going home
and how we sat there,
clinical and broken hearted.
It's true that grief has a way
of stabbing you in the back.

But now I look out over the river,
the water is flowing through my hands
as if I had always belonged here,
my arm through yours.
Black angels fill the sky,
we watch the past becoming the future,
day slowing sliding into night.
There are violins of shooting stars,
the rain has never been so sweet.

Boats

We drive to Dun Laoghaire
with your two year old and your baby in the back.
It's late but they're wide awake,
so much for the hope the rhythm of the car wheels
would give them better dreams.

You curse the cost of the double buggy
as you open out it's complicated machinery.
All those wheels within wheels.
I think, you could invade Baghdad with that,
as we head off down the pier, moving fast,
'cos though the kids have hats and blankets
you've forgotten your jacket.

You tell me how your mother has pneumonia
and the antibiotics aren't working,
they think they'll have to operate,
and how your 18 year old cousin committed suicide,
and how they overpaid your husband by mistake
but now the money's gone
and you've no way to pay it back.

The ships wink their tiny lights far out to sea
as your two year old claps his hands with delight.
Yes, you say to him, *boats, aren't they great*.
You sound tired, as if the Irish Sea
were pressing on your shoulders,
and I wish for a moment we could sail away.

But then you smile and tell me,
he's got new words every day.
And your son takes your hand,
and the baby has fallen asleep,
and I only turn back once to look at the boats.
Such strange currents, unknown lighthouses,
the mystery of so much water.

Hospice

We waited,
listening to the radio

clinging to familiar voices,
traffic reports,

weather bulletins,
proof there was still a world out there.

You sat in your ironed pyjamas
drinking tea with five sugars

and death took his time,
his own sweet time.

Journey

The train rolls out from under a cloud
as the mountains give way to sun baked
orchids in terracotta swirls. The sea flashes past
with its promise of sailing boats and chocolate beaches.

A single purple shirt hung from a balcony
waving in defiance,
connections that have not been missed.
A white square of sunshine, coffee with milk,
a large triumphant fountain.
The whole of France passing under wheels
and the surprise of such warmth,
the couple across from me, so clearly in love,
pronouncing this the only way to travel.

I could, after all these years,
still get off at any stop I choose.
There are beginnings
and there are homecomings,
coins in my pocket,
my passport on the fold out table,
the world passing my window,
I remain somehow this reflection of a stranger.

Why I love train journeys

Sometimes
I suspect
happiness
is not at all what
we have been taught
to believe it is.

Instead
it can be found
in between destinations,
moments of unbearable beauty
that catch the breath
with their sudden magic
and are gone.

Vienna

The rows of concrete books,
unreadable atrocities, the erasing of faces,
even the animals had to be sewn back together.
Gods smashed to pieces, the desecration
of graveyards or just the simple lack of flowers.
No ghosts to tend these ghetto memories.
The peeling of generations.
Wiesenthal saved by the bell.
Other slaughtered prayers.

In the rumbling of coffee houses,
the vast silences of so much savagery,
Bosnian war crimes, the hatred of gypsies,
the man in the market still saying he is from Yugoslavia.
To come from a place that no longer exists,
to step into a future with Nazi credentials,
call it immigration, call it economics,
call it a blossoming between gravestones,
the courage to come back.

Such heavy set grandeur,
Freud and his impossible dreams,
Wittgenstein giving up philosophy
to take a lover forty years younger.
Under this solid politeness, the frankly met gazes,
the professor asking about African spears,
Rastafarian kidnappings, refusing
to believe in a black classical composer.

And all around the snow capped peaks
of unspeakable beauty. So much whiteness,
a sugar coating on a darkness
that still breathes through
sixty thousand Jewish whispers.

Miles Davis said to John Coltrane...

as he went on and on
into the early hours of the morning
burning himself up
with all that jazz,
too many ideas spinning through him,
too many notes and not enough time,
too much genius, too much soul,
not knowing when to call it a night,
not able to stop himself, *try taking*
the mothafucka out of your mouth,
such simple good advice.

Birth

Cool was born in the smoky backrooms
of small bars with the whisky tinkling
into glasses, the piano put on ice,
the low slow groan of a saxophone
splitting open the night
and all those notes spilling out onto the pavement.

Some crazy jigsaw cracked into blue pieces of sex
and heroin and too many weeks on the road,
the sweat of souls set free, a certain clarity,
a black and white world where you could lose
yourself in the shades of grey, where the chances
of a man falling down a flight of stairs
were proportional to the colour of his skin.
Where did all those needles come from anyway?
The opium dreams of a new kind of slavery,
addicted to criminalisation,
play the music, ban the musician.

Dark, dangerous, the devil's promise.
Who built these crossroads?
In the deep blood rivers of Alabama,
in the arteries of Africa,
in the spiritual grace of these invisible chains
the blues can be broken, spun and woven
into rainbows of trumpets burning with the intensity
of angels putting cigarettes out on your skin.

Just under the polished surface
there's a whole revolution
simmering and swirling, sweeping
back the boundaries of the night.

Mass

Deep in the belly of candlelit ruins,
the fragments of reflecting glass,
holy water glistening,
not sure how to bless myself
I murmur made up words
Whole macaroni bless be the tide
in the fruit of her room all men.
Stand up, sit down,
like jumping jacks.
Mysterious and bewildering,
lost languages,
my grandmother's intensity.

We'd stroll back
through lanes full of butterflies,
their wings gossamer thin,
the sun tipping the world into our faces.
This too I felt was somehow God.
No words to pin us to a board,
just light and summer
and her hand in mine,
old but swinging.

Fashion statement

I would like to be dressed
in the gold of Christmas chocolate coins,
my hair pinned up with candy canes,
my eyes coated with emeralds,
my tongue pierced with diamonds
and on each of my fingers,
a ruby red enough to draw blood.

My fingernails would be painted
all the colours of the Sistine Chapel,
and my smile only Mona Lisa could share.
I'd have boots made for stomping,
with killer sex kitten heels
and toes reinforced with steel.
Around my neck I'd wear a boa constrictor,
a real one, with a poisonous bite, but I'd avoid furs.

Instead my coat would be purple velvet
and stretch out for miles behind me,
I'd line it with secret kisses
and wild nights out on the town.
I'd have earrings made from beer bottle caps
and a champagne cork inserted into my navel.

On my ankles I'd tattoo the names of my dreams
so that I never forget them, and my stockings
would run ladders of newspaper headlines
so that everyone would know
why I was fashionably late.

I'd have a corset made from plastic bubble wrap
and petticoats sewn from red roses.
My dress would be cut from snowflakes,
the kind you find inside crystal balls,
and it would fit me like a second skin
sliding over me soft as mercury
so that I rippled as I walked
and I'd be silver and shiny and endlessly skinny.

I'd wear a belt studded with bullets
and carry a dagger, long and cruel,
and I'd sport a sailor's cap
with a phoenix feather tucked into it
so that when I rose from the ashes
of your indifference,
all post punk indie waif glamour queen,
we'd see if you dared not to notice.

Conscience

In the city of lost children
kidnapped from the roots of trees,
the shadows are hunting.
A handprint on a wall,
the fading of blood,
the graffiti of the missing.

You too can disappear here;
in the silence of the torture chambers,
the buried screams, unheard confessions,
broken signatures, the erasing of hope,
footsteps echoing down glass corridors,
mirrors with no faces.

Tell yourself this isn't your world;
gold chains bruised around necks,
diamond Kalashnikovs,
smiles of oil, dangerous experiments.
In the dancing of the television,
the peddling of fear,
the growth of suicide,
is their face more covered than yours?

Advice

We're in the kitchen making dinner and the steam is covering the windows and I'm writing my name and she tells me to stop, it'll leave marks, and she's small but she's not to be messed with. She's telling a story about my uncle and how he never would have left home if she hadn't packed for him and helped him find the flat 'cos you got to stand on your own feet in this world, can't be hiding behind doors waiting for love to arrive. Whose gonna love you if you're still living at home with your mother? A year later he was married.

I'm ten years old and I'm sitting on a high red stool and stirring the gravy, only half listening because I've heard this story before. The strip light is on in the window and we can see the light of my Dad's bike coming up the path. It's cold and wet and we're inside and it's time to set the table. She says get the knives and forks from the wooden drawer. I wipe down the counter with a blue J-cloth, kicking over the dog's water bowl so the brown tiled carpet is wet and she says can't you do anything right?

So I ask her a question because this is philosophy hour but it's hard not to let it get to you. It's only years later her words come back to me in their infinite wisdom because you have to accept people for what they are. There's courage in responsibility, for seeing that it might be me that needs changing. There was always a warmth in her warnings, which maybe I didn't get at the time, but now I hold close as the shadow of my name scrawled on the window, because she was right, it did leave a mark.